A HEAVY BOOK FOR ALL AGES

JAESOP

Copyright © 2020 by Jaesop

All rights reserved.

No part of this book may be reproduced in any form or by any electronic or mechanical means, including information storage and retrieval systems, without written permission from the author, except for the use of brief quotations in a book review.

CONTENTS

Preface ... 1

PART I
ASKING

WHAT DO I WANT?	9
1. Inner craving	10
2. Object of desire	12
3. Safety	14
4. Participation	16
5. Experience as a determinant of wants	18
6. Belief as a determinant of wants	20
7. Budget as a determinant of wants	22
8. Influence	24
9. Support/ guidance / mistrust/ contrarianism	26
10. Instinct/ subversion /obedience/ repression	28
11. Acquired tastes/ brainwashing/ single-mindedness/ self-assertion	30
12. For kicks/ curiosity/ don't give a damn/ passivity	32
13. Aphrodisiac/ empty wants	34
14. Addiction/ self-control	36
WHAT DO I NEED TO KNOW?	39
15. The objects of knowledge: experiences, facts, laws, etc.	40
16. Education: relevant or a distraction	42
17. Knowledge depends on the reliability of its source	44

18. People have wants, experiences, beliefs, budgets (skills, assets), position; they decide, act and seek to influence	46
19. People try to influence others' experiences, beliefs, budgets and hence their wants to try to get what they want	48
20. People provide incorrect and irrelevant information about the world in order to influence others' beliefs to try to get what they want	50
21. People (mis)represent themselves and others in order to influence others and try to get what they want	52
22. Self-knowledge is elusive	54
23. Possibility of change: nature, nurture, or choice	56
24. Feelings	58

WHAT DO I NEED TO HAVE?	61
25. Ability as a combination of experience, knowledge, talent, and practice	62
26. Valuable abilities	64
27. The limits of ability	66
28. Ability to get to know others: question, research, empathise, observe, probe, spy and introspect	68
29. Showing: communicating without talking	70
30. Showing-off and proof of ability	72
31. Talking without communicating	74
32. Ability to collaborate with others	76
33. Ability to gain access, develop a reputation, and get selected	78
34. Assets affect our experience, beliefs, practice, and hence our abilities	80
35. Space, materials and tools are needed to do things	82
36. You don't need much to dream	84
37. Immaterial property contracts	86

38. Credit (advances and deferrals)	88
39. Options	90
40. Time	92

PART II
DOING

WHAT CAN I DO?	97
41. Consume or produce	98
42. Gathering	100
43. Making	102
44. Providing service	104
45. Managing/ supervising	106
46. Searching	108
47. Promoting/ selling	110
48. Trading/negotiating	112
49. Begging/ getting something for nothing (giving)	114
50. Taking	116
51. Teaching/corrupting	118
52. Leading/aggregating from the poor	120
WHAT SHOULD I DO?	123
53. Paralysis	124
54. Intentional inaction	126
55. Less responsibility, less effort, less failure	128
56. More reliable more protected	130
57. Habit, tradition and convention	132
58. Deciding	134
59. Taking risks and success	136
60. Savings and sacrifice	138
61. Performing	140
62. Rules and ethics	142
63. Bullies and power	144

PART III
RECOGNISING

WHY DO I COMPLAIN?	149
64. Unfairness	150
65. Criticism and failure	152
66. Partial success	154
67. Getting back on your feet	156
WHY DO I CELEBRATE?	159
68. Celebration as acknowledgment	160
69. Partying	162

PREFACE

I remember being a young child. Like many children, I asked myself questions. I noticed early on that some people do not behave nicely. I thought it was because they were not very smart, or because they were bad. I felt that by asking myself the right questions I could find a way for all of us to be happy.

I realised later that achieving this is not so straightforward. People often find that being nice to others is not rewarding. Perhaps this is the reason why many people drift towards thinking only about their own interests, despite being taught from an early age to care for others.

Whatever the reasons may be, a world driven by self-interest is complicated and full of suspicion. Learning in such a world is difficult, and it is easy to get lost. Ideally, we are taught by trusted people, whether by example or by being taught facts and rules. But how can we know that what we are taught is right if people don't really care about us? We can't.

This means that we need to learn to think for ourselves while we learn from others. It is hard work and takes time. It is like putting together the pieces of a puzzle. It is especially hard if you start the puzzle from the wrong place, if some pieces are missing, or worse still, if they are being hidden from you.

One day I decided I would share some clues of how I think such a puzzle can be put together in the hope that they might help others in the same way that they could have helped me. So I set about writing these stories.

These stories are peculiar. I like to think of them as pointing to the pieces that matter most. I have chosen them as I would artefacts in a museum. Their aim is to show the familiar in a brighter light and so provide a framework with which to interpret events in the world. They do not aim to give answers or tell you what to do. You will have to look for answers elsewhere.

Even today, I find it quite striking how reluctant older people are to teach younger ones, especially things that cannot be learned at school. Sometimes I think it is because they are not sure or because they don't like what they have learnt. Other times I think of more sinister or selfish motives. Regardless of the answer, I encourage you to discuss these 'multilogues' with teachers, friends, or relatives. I would treat them simply as the starting point of a discussion.

Learning takes courage, and you are often on your own. It will probably be awkward at times, a sure sign you are near an uncomfortable truth.

Note:

Every multilogue relates to a place on the map on p.5. One starts by asking, then doing and finally recognising the results of one's actions, and then starting over again, under the purvue of others' wants.

Our four speakers Ani (A), Eli (E), Shah (H) and Suki (S) are really placeholders and not characters with overarching character traits. Any of us could be any of them at a given moment in time.

MAP

PART I
ASKING

WHAT DO I WANT?

I WANT TO …

1. Inner craving

W(I1)

A: I want to eat

E: How can you tell?

A: I sense it in my tummy

H: I just heard it rumble

S: I can tell you are hungry because you are grumpy

E: And you don't even realise you are

H: Sometimes I want to eat even if I am not hungry

E: Like when you go past the cookie jar

2. Object of desire

W(I2)

E: I want those shoes

H: I like them! They are beautiful

S: It must feel nice to walk in them

A: They won't help you run faster though

E: I think I look great in them

A: They might hide your ugly feet but not your ugly face

E: At least I can show I can afford them

H: If I owned them, I would look at them every day

A: You just want what others have

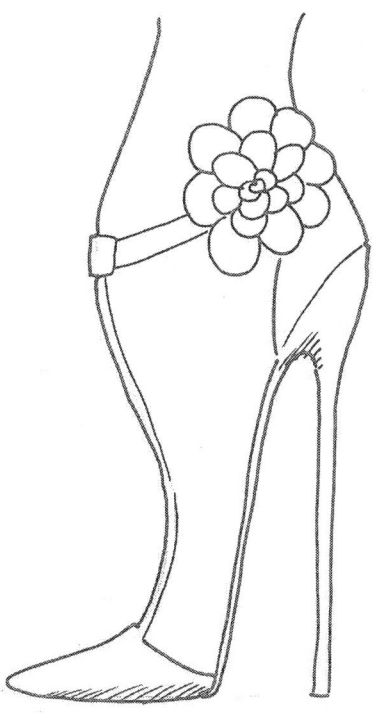

3. Safety

W(I3)

H: I want to be safe in my neighbourhood

S: Then leave your gold chain in the safe

A: Or just hide in the cellar

E: You could catch a cold down there

H: I don't feel safe when no one is looking after me

S: It is just as dangerous to be with us

A: Eli often hurts me by calling me names

E: If you do as I say, I will protect you

H: I would rather get mugged than do as you say

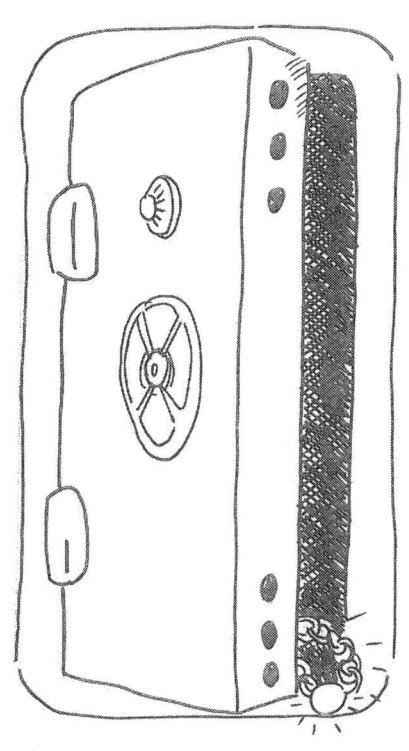

4. Participation

W(I4)

S: I want to play

A: Play with your toys

S: I want to play with real people

E: We don't want you in our crew, you are useless

A: We could let him be our assistant

E: Or he can just watch us on TV

A: What shall we do, Shah?

H: Leave me alone! Can't you see I am trying to play with Suki?

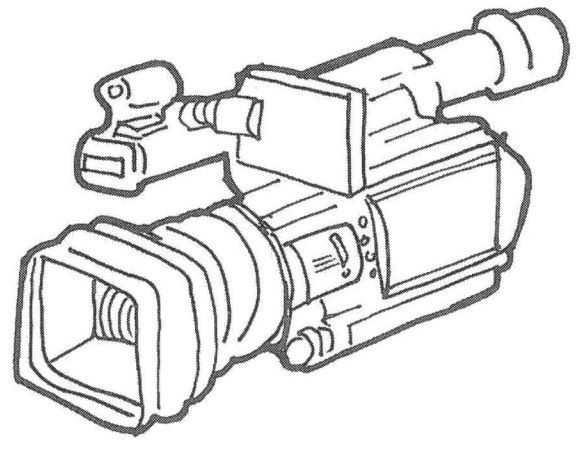

… BUT THERE ARE DETERMINANTS

5. Experience as a determinant of wants

W(I,D1)

A: It's the first time I've seen a cat like that

E: I am not touching anything that I haven't touched before

S: Unless you pet it, you won't know if you like it

H: I got scratched last time I got near one

E: You might be allergic too

A: I like how it feels

S: It feels horrible

A: She's licking my hand! I am keeping her

6. Belief as a determinant of wants

W(I,D2)

E: The Moon is great to visit

H: I had never thought of going there

A: I've heard it's horribly cold

H: I want to go!

S: Travelling is not good for you

H: I find that hard to believe

A: So you listen to Eli and not to me

H: I have full faith in astronauts

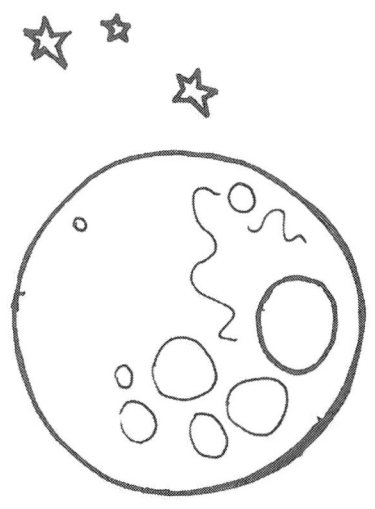

7. Budget as a determinant of wants

W(I,D3)

H: Can I play tennis with you?

S: You are not a club member

E: And you don't play well enough

A: Perhaps you can practice and ask again

H: I don't have the time to practice

A: If I were a better player, I would ask someone else

H: Anyway, I didn't want to play in the first place

S: You know you want to

8. Influence

Our experiences, beliefs, budgets and hence our wants, are influenced by others who may want us to want certain things so they can try to get what they want

W(I,D(U))

S: I told you I don't want to take care of the rabbit

A: I thought if you saw him, you would change your mind

H: Believe us, having a pet will cheer you up

E: I will bring you carrots; you only have to feed him for a week

S: OK I'll do it for you, but you owe me

E: By next week, you'll beg us to keep him

S: He is very sweet!

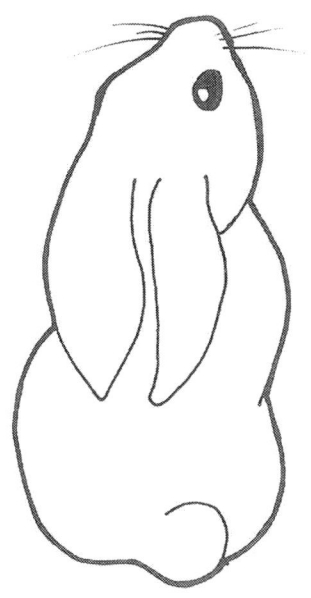

9. Support/ guidance / mistrust/ contrarianism

W(I,D(U))/ W(D(U),I) /~ W(I,D(U))/ ~W(D(U),I)

A: You may want to put your hat on

H: Good idea; the sun is very hot!

S: Are you sure a bee isn't hiding in it?

E: Maybe Ani wants you to get stung

A: I was trying to be helpful

E: She's always wrong, so I want the opposite of what she suggests

S: Eli, you just don't like being told what to do

10. Instinct/ subversion /obedience/ repression

W(I,D(~U))/   W(D(~U),I)   /   ~W(I,D(~U))/ ~W(D(~U),I)

E: I feel like dancing

S: Stop behaving like a wild animal

E: What's wrong with dancing?

A: You will hurt yourself

H: You are jealous of how well she dances

S: Let me turn the music down

E: Thanks for that! I was getting carried away

11. Acquired tastes/ brainwashing/ single-mindedness/ self-assertion

W(~I,D(U))/   W(D(U),~I)   /~   W(~I,D(U))/ ~W(D(U),~I)

H: Drink the fish-liver oil

A: No! It tastes horrible

E: You will like it after a couple of times

H: It has nutrients that are good for you

A: OK, if you say so

S: Are you trying to poison us?

A: Now I'm really not drinking it!

12. For kicks/ curiosity/ don't give a damn/ passivity

W(~I,D(~U))/   W(D(~U),~I)   /~   W(~I,D(~U))/ ~W(D(~U),~I)

S: I don't want to go outside

E: These beds are so comfortable

A: There is no point in you leaving the house

S: I should do something

H: There is nothing worth doing in this village

S: Let's go to the mall. We might get some ideas

H: OK. You never know

13. Aphrodisiac/ empty wants

W(~I,D(U),WW))/ ~W(~I,D(U),WW)

A: I want to be hungry again

H: Why aren't you?

A: I am sick

H: If you take some medicine, your appetite will come back

E: Are you sure that's the best cure?

S: Maybe you are not hungry

A: It is no fun not feeling like anything

S: Being hungry and having nothing to eat is no fun either

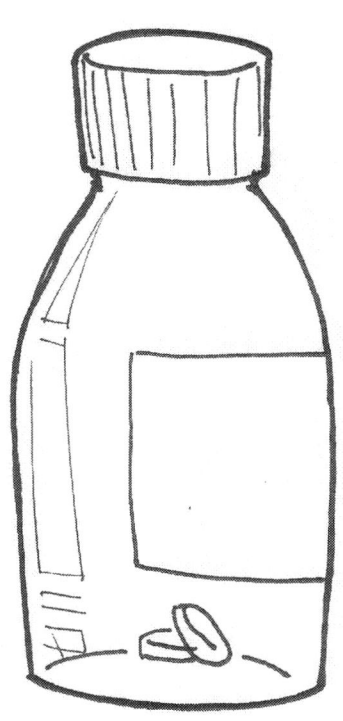

14. Addiction/ self-control

W(~I,D(U),~WW))/ ~W(~I,D(U),~WW)

E: Why are you scratching?

S: I am very itchy

E: If you keep doing it, you will get a scar

S: I can't help it. It's so difficult to resist the urge

H: Even though I would rather not, scratching is a relief

A: I don't give in to temptation

E: I sometimes choose to

WHAT DO I NEED TO KNOW?

ABOUT THE WORLD

15. The objects of knowledge: experiences, facts, laws, etc.

H: What do I need to know to warm up?

A: That there is a dog by the bench

S: And that if you huddle against it, you will feel warmer

H: It's cozy! I couldn't have guessed

E: That's why experience is necessary

A: You could also have worked that out if you had known that a dog's temperature is higher than yours

S: And that if a body has a higher temperature than another, it transfers heat to it

H: Will I feel warmer if I huddle against a lion?

E: You might well feel a chill down your spine

16. Education: relevant or a distraction

S: Please learn the words to this song

E: Last time you didn't even test us

H: I enjoy memorising lyrics

E: Can you smell something burning?

A: I learn more playing around a bonfire than in this class

S: To be in the choir, you need to know them

E: I think the fire alarm needs repairing

H: Run for the exit or we'll get roasted!

17. Knowledge depends on the reliability of its source

A: I think the neighbour kidnaps children

S: Who told you?

A: Let's ask Shah. He knows these things

E: Shah hasn't checked if bones are buried next door

A: He might know someone who has

S: Maybe the neighbour started the rumour

H: The neighbour wouldn't know whom to tell

A: I am pulling your leg! I made the story up

ABOUT PEOPLE

18. People have wants, experiences, beliefs, budgets (skills, assets), position; they decide, act and seek to influence

E: Why is Suki holding a knife?

A: Maybe he wants to hurt us

H: Perhaps he has seen wolves in the forest

A: Surely he can't believe he can fend them off with a pocket knife

E: He's smiling and holding it too loosely to want to use it

H: If a wolf showed up, I think he would choose to run

A: His feet would run before he had time to think

S: Don't laugh. I am trying to look menacing!

19. People try to influence others' experiences, beliefs, budgets and hence their wants to try to get what they want

(see 8, page 24)

20. People provide incorrect and irrelevant information about the world in order to influence others' beliefs to try to get what they want

S: The fountain of happiness is on that hilltop

H: Eli, buy my walking stick. It will help you to get there safely

A: Eli, give me your drink. You won't need it up there

S: Eli, carry me to the foothill, and I will show you the way

E: I am now penniless, thirsty and tired. The three of you are smiling, and there is no fountain to be found

H: You may be penniless, but the exercise has made you strong and healthy

A: You may be thirsty, but you have discovered a beautiful view

S: You may be tired, but you have a new friend in me

21. People (mis)represent themselves and others in order to influence others and try to get what they want

A: You are so handsome

S: I do my best to look good

H: She doesn't think you are handsome. She just wants to hold your hand because you are wearing a beautiful polo shirt

A: If you were friendlier, Shah, I would say nice things about you

E: Shah doesn't dress well because he only wants certain people to know how great he is

H: By dressing casually. I find it easier to get to know what others are like

S: Well, Shah might think he is special, but he is a bad person

E: Now you lie about Shah because you are scared that Ani might like Shah more than you

S: At least I don't pretend he doesn't exist

ABOUT MYSELF

22. Self-knowledge is elusive

S: I am not sure I am a good gymnast

E: Have you looked in the mirror?

H: Use a video camera and you won't need to keep your head still while you look

S: I guess that I am doing well when I feel coordinated

A: Your legs were all over the place

E: Ani, you are too tough!

S: I don't like video footage of myself

H: But, Suki, you have won gold! Maybe tomorrow you will see things differently

23. Possibility of change: nature, nurture, or choice

H: I want to be an ogre

E: You can't be; either you are one or you are not

S: If you continue to eat junk food, you will end up looking like one

A: The shape of your skull won't change though

E: You do have the personality of an ogre

H: People have damaged me. That is why I have become this way

S: You just got into a bad habit and can be friendly if you try

A: You just like being nasty!

24. Feelings

S: I feel weird in this cave

H: Perhaps you just want to be back home

E: Is it a strange smell or did you hear something?

S: I will start screaming if we don't go

H: You feel anxious for no reason

A: Look at the bats hanging up there!

S: Run! I am so embarrassed about being such a coward

A: I am relieved we are back in the open too

S: You'll think I am mad, but I feel we need to go back

WHAT DO I NEED TO HAVE?

ABILITIES

25. Ability as a combination of experience, knowledge, talent, and practice

A: I am learning musical notes so I can rock this town!

E: Can you play any chords?

A: Not yet but I know where they are on the guitar

H: I could play a bit on my first day

S: You'll need more practice to find out how good you are

E: A teacher will help you to learn faster

H: Nothing beats experimenting with others

S: That's a cool sound! Even you don't know what you are doing

26. Valuable abilities

E: I am working on a new pizza formula to impress Shah

H: Why bother? Frozen ones are cheap and easy to prepare

S: But I don't like them

A: Yours looks difficult to make

S: It tastes delicious! You will make a fortune from this recipe

H: Eli, shall we eat your pizza and watch a film together?

A: By tomorrow Shah will be bored of you

E: Not tonight though

27. The limits of ability

H: I can't move my ears

S: Some of us can and some of us can't

A: I can't move my wings because I don't have any

E: We build planes so that we can fly

S: With practice, you can become a pilot

E: You make that sound so easy

S: It is!

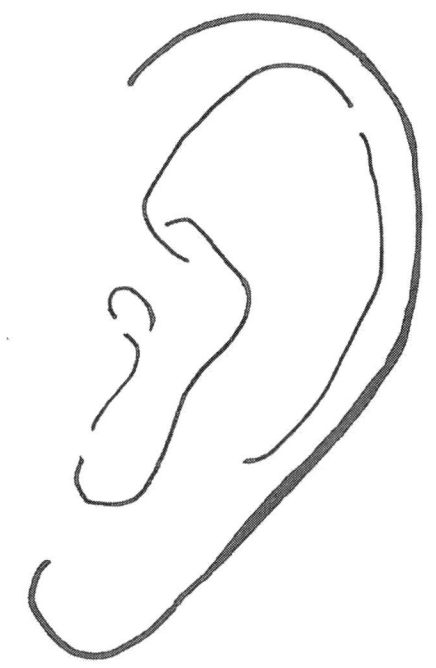

28. Ability to get to know others: question, research, empathise, observe, probe, spy and introspect

S: Are you ready for the big game?

A: Of course I am

E: I read in the news that you fell off your bike

H: Are you feeling sore? I felt a lot of pain when I fell

S: You are limping and have a huge bruise!

A: Ouch, don't press!

E: Actually I have been spying on you and saw you fall badly

S: Let's get you checked by the doctor or you are not playing

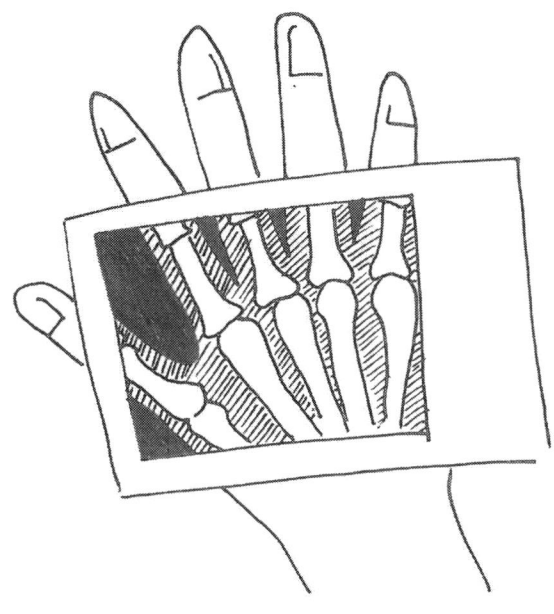

29. Showing: communicating without talking

A: Suki, that's a big chef hat you are wearing

E: He is the boss in the kitchen

S: Eli, let me show you how to chop the onions

E: Shah, stop pretending you are busy and come and help

S: Shah, don't stick your tongue out at Eli!

H: Don't cry, Eli

E: It's because of the onions

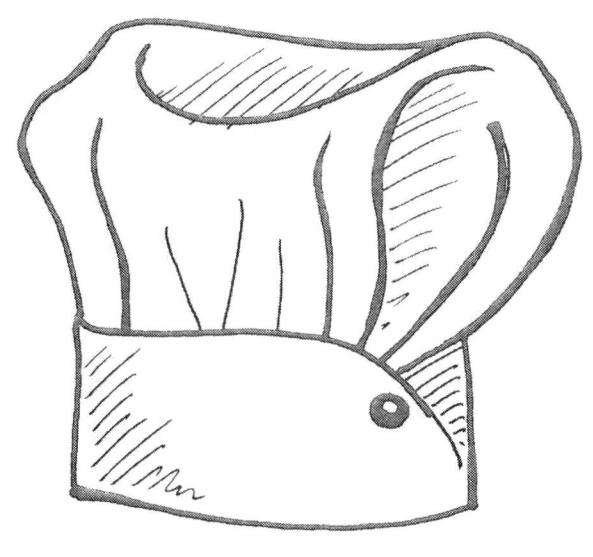

30. Showing-off and proof of ability

E: I saw a man in the street swallow a sword

H: Why bother to do that?

E: I guess it's proof of bravery

A: I love swallowing fish bones

E: Go ahead; show me

A: I need to save them for the cat

S: Your word is no proof

H: She usually does what she says she will do

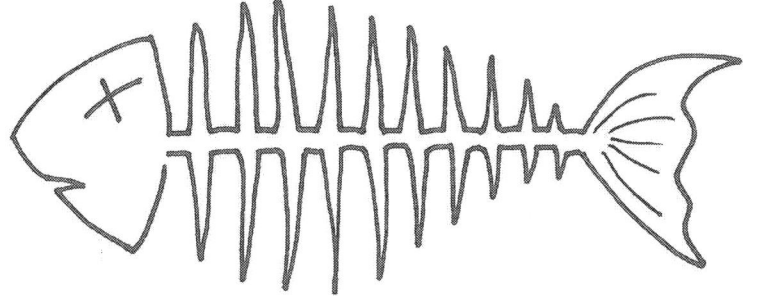

31. Talking without communicating

H: I think you guys are clowns

S: Are you trying to start a fight?

H: Not really; I just thought I would say something

A: Think before you speak then

S: Someone bring me earplugs

E: He's trying to be friendly and get our attention

H: Loosen up

32. Ability to collaborate with others

S: What are you doing?

A: I am trying to climb the wall to capture the enemy flag

S: Stand on my shoulders

H: Don't bother. Eli is on the wall and will push you away

A: We should be patient. She might take a nap

S: Listen, while you speak with Eli, Ani can climb on my shoulders

E: Guys, I can see everything you are doing

S: Now! Grab her ankle and bring her down!

33. Ability to gain access, develop a reputation, and get selected

A: Can I board your boat?

H: We didn't invite you. How did you find us?

A: I looked for the biggest boat in the harbour

S: She is dressed like a pirate, so we should let her in

H: That doesn't mean she won't get seasick

E: I've seen her sail before

H: If we let you join the crew, will you do as told or will you just lie around?

E: If we don't vote her in, she might start her own crew

ASSETS

34. Assets affect our experience, beliefs, practice, and hence our abilities

(also our wants; see 7, page 22)

E: Let's water ski

S: We need a speedboat for that

A: This is hard; I keep falling over

S: If you owned a boat, you would be able to practice more

E: Thanks to skiing, I saw my first dolphin

H: If you want to see fish, just go to the aquarium

A: Shah, the only fish you have seen is at the fishmongers

E: I take care of dolphins every summer now

35. Space, materials and tools are needed to do things

H: I'd like to build a car so I don't have to walk to school

A: There's a car here

H: Yes, but it's not ours, and we don't have the right to use it

E: Let's get some old tires from the garage

S: Do we have a place where we can build it?

E: We have paper, scissors and string

H: We need a list of the parts, who supplies them, assembly equipment, and an instruction manual. And money to pay for it

A: Shall we just buy one?

36. You don't need much to dream

S: I've spent all morning under a tree imagining I am flying a private jet

E: Any plans to make your dream come true?

A: It will take more than a summer internship

H: It takes too much time to be able to afford one

S: The thought is nice though

H: In dreams you don't need to pass a flying test either

E: I will work for it! The real world has lots to offer!

A: You are such a dreamer

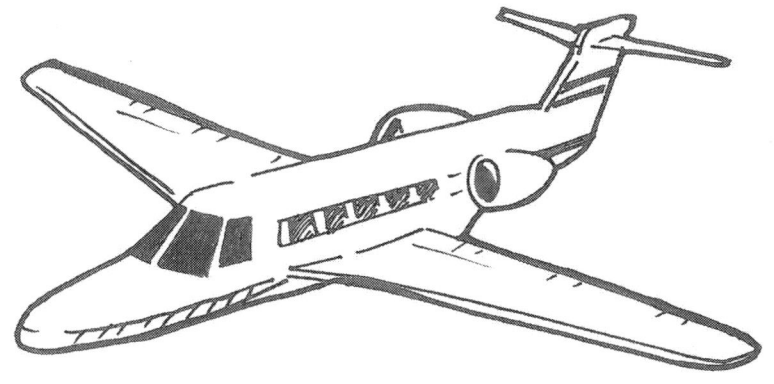

37. Immaterial property contracts

A: I know a mix of herbs that smells great

H: Will you tell me what it is?

A: I don't want to share that information

E: She has spent a lot of time working on it

S: If you tell us, we won't tell others

H: And we won't produce the mix for others

A: Put it in a contract and sign

E: Let's agree or she won't invent in the future

38. Credit (advances and deferrals)

E: I would like to set up a lemonade stand

S: Shah has lemons in his orchard

H: The lemons are mine

A: Lend them to Eli, and she can pay you back once she has sold some lemonade

H: Can I let you know in a few days?

A: I can't wait to have one of your lemonades

E: If I don't set the stand up now, I will miss the opportunity

S: Run into the garden and just take some

39. Options

H: Are you coming to the picnic?

A: Maybe

S: Ani, what are you giving us to have that choice?

A: The chance of my presence is enough

H: Great, and on top of it all, I always end up cooking

E: I will be there for sure and will sing for you

A: Even if I do come, if I don't like the picnic, I will leave

H: Please do not come then

40. Time

S: I am writing a book

E: Aren't you busy writing this week's essay?

H: He is very efficient and has already finished

A: Plus he has been writing on the bus for many months

E: I have to work most of the time and hardly get to sleep

A: I am exhausted after work

H: With your savings you can afford to take time off

S: I work hard now so I have time later

PART II
DOING

WHAT CAN I DO?

WHAT CAN I DO?

41. Consume or produce

A: Let's have a milkshake

S: I don't have any money

E: Ani gets money given to her

A: My focus is on how to spend it, which is not easy!

S: I have to deliver milk boxes to survive

E: Logistics is an interesting field

H: Ani doesn't even know that milk is shipped from warehouses to shops

A: I guess I just make people happy by being me

42. Gathering

E: I am gathering blackberries by the river

A: So we don't need to grow them

H: The supermarket is closer

S: And they already come in a box

A: You will have to dig deep to pay for them

H: We don't own any land

S: Let's claim the river area as ours

E: I'll gather everyone and let them know

43. Making

H: I would like to sleep in a treehouse

E: I can design and build one for you

A: Let's make planks out of those trees

S: We do have a saw

A: Good, as I wouldn't be able to make a steel blade

E: Has anyone ever seen what a machine that makes blades looks like?

S: And how would *that* machine be made?

H: Imagine if we had to start from scratch

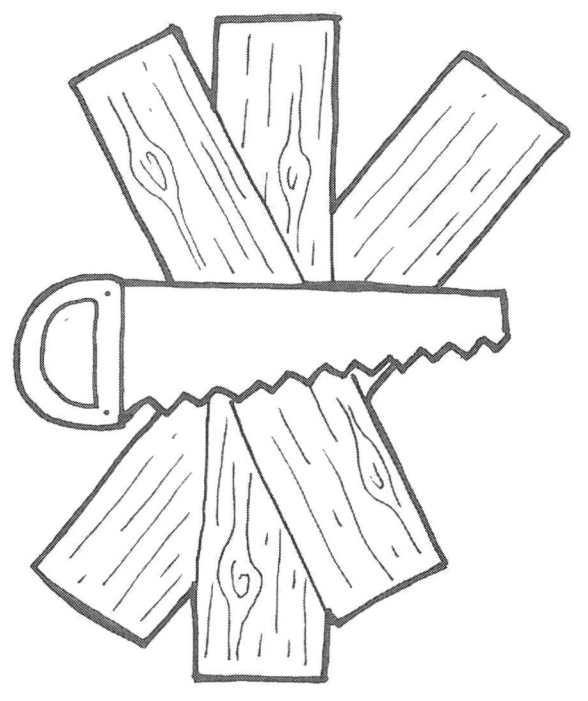

44. Providing service

S: I need to wash my hair

H: Will it be easier if Ani helps you?

A: I'll do it for you if you wash mine later

E: I am happy to do it for nothing

A: You just like playing with Suki's hair

S: But Eli, you are very rough with my hair

E: I'll make you look good

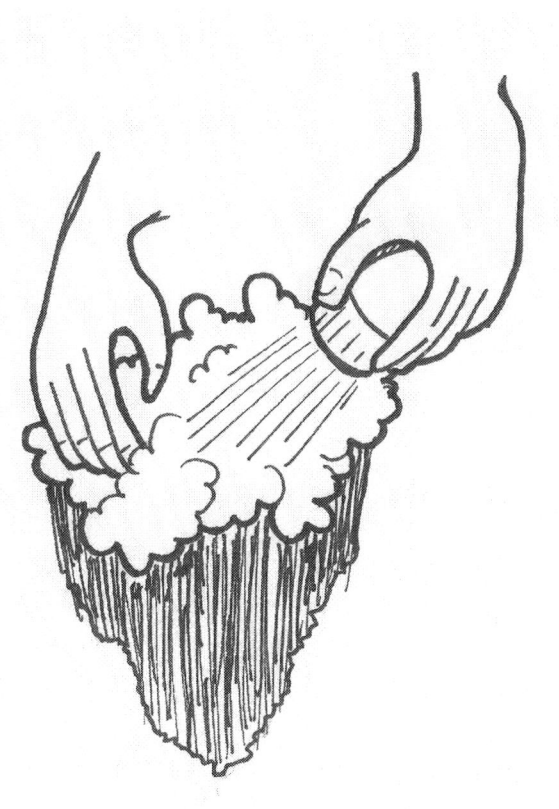

45. Managing/ supervising

A: Do we want to win this match?

S: I am tired of not scoring

H: I've been watching you, and you need improvement

S: Let's find someone better for my position

E: Suki, you are lazy and bossy

H: I think Suki's a better coach than player

A: We need to get rid of him

S: Now look who's bossy

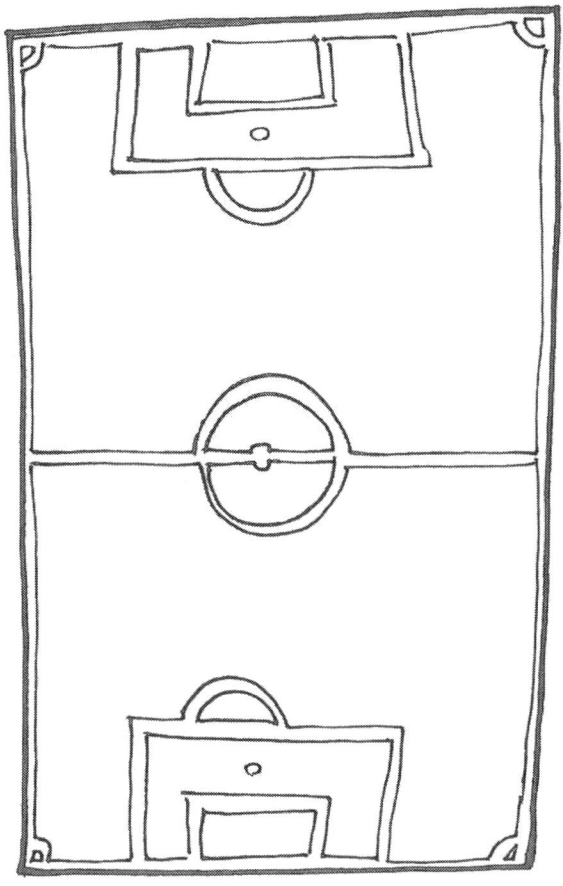

46. Searching

E: What are you looking for?

A: I don't know

S: I am looking for a golden flute in the sand

E: How do you know it is there?

S: If I find it, it will be mine

E: Let's search on the web for a place to eat

A: Let's find a spot to lie down while he digs

E: Good idea; I have finished my lab research for the day

H: Here you are! I was looking for you

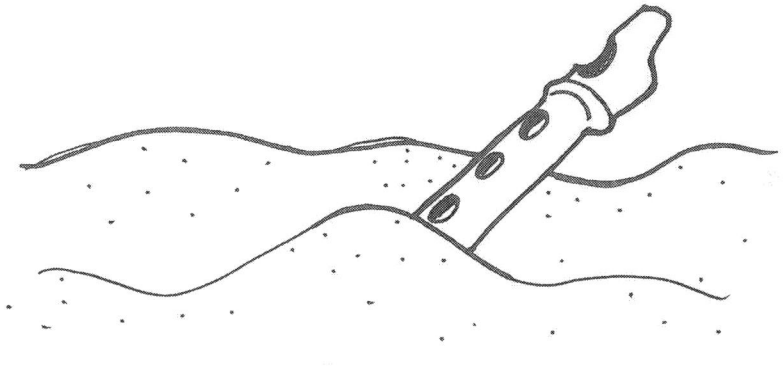

47. Promoting/ selling

H: Come into my shop!

E: Why do you need to shout?

H: We have a special sale on

S: This dress is really nice. I hadn't noticed it

H: It's made of very soft fabric

A: It's nice now, but you haven't mentioned if it discolours after washing

S: I like you and the dress; I'll take it

H: Great purchase, come back soon!

48. Trading/negotiating

S: We bought this drawing in the market

H: I can see it's a drawing I made

E: The lady didn't know who it's by; that's why we bought it cheap

A: She was in a rush to sell

S: If we auction it, we will get a much higher price

E: If it weren't for me, you wouldn't have noticed it

A: I got her to reduce the price by half

S: I paid for it, but we can discuss how to share the profit

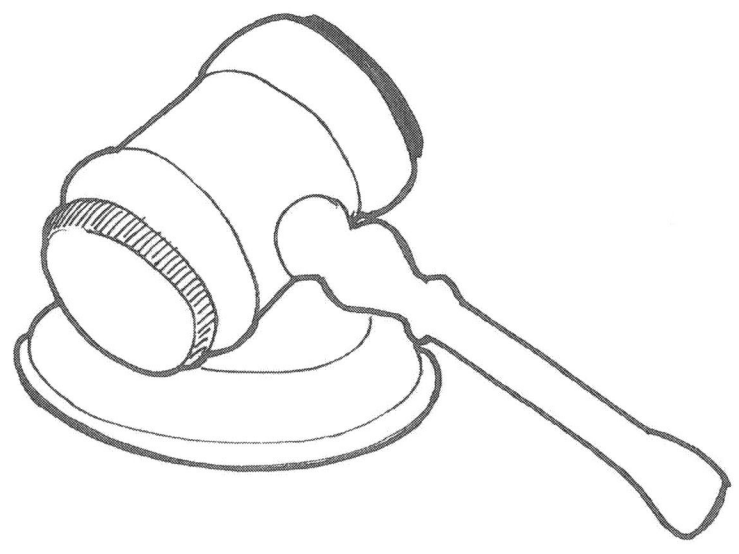

49. Begging/ getting something for nothing (giving)

A: Eli is back from hospital

E: Ani has taken care of me

H: Eli, do you ever go into work?

A: I am organising a charity event to help pay the bill

S: Don't bother me with your problems

E: If one day you are sick, we will help you

S: I pay taxes so I don't have to beg

H: I pay taxes so others don't have to work

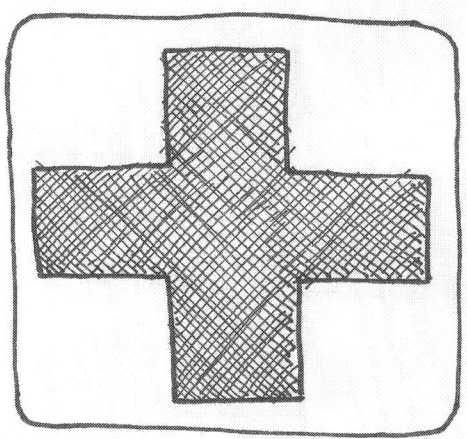

50. Taking

E: Give me your pencil case!

H: I don't want to

S: If you don't, Eli will take it from you

H: But it's mine

A: If you don't, she will twist your arm

H: I will call the teacher, and she will send you to detention

E: She's my friend and won't stop me

H: I'll get my revenge one day

51. Teaching/corrupting

H: We are so lucky that you explain things to us

S: And that you show us how to live a good life

A: Let's skip class, eat junk food and smoke

E: Ani, why do you want us to do that?

H: She wants to make money by selling us cigarettes, even if it hurts us

A: Doesn't my big car prove that I know best?

S: I won't lead a bad life in order to afford a car like yours

E: Suki, aren't you exaggerating a bit?

52. Leading/aggregating from the poor

S: Can we have some water?

A: No

S: Hey everyone, can you help me to buy equipment to drill a well?

E: Great idea!

H: Agreed; how much of the water will you keep?

A: Suki, if you don't drill the well, I'll give you some water

E: I prefer to get water from the new well

S: Ani, you can drink all your water yourself

WHAT SHOULD I DO?

NOT DO ANYTHING

53. Paralysis

A: Lying on the hammock is paradise

E: We should be preparing for the hurricane

S: I don't know how to

E: Maybe we should board the windows

A: I can't see how that will help

H: I am not sure there is much that we can do

S: The thought is so depressing

E: Come on; we must think of something

54. Intentional inaction

E: Shhh, don't make any noise!

H: We don't want the tiger to see us

A: He is going to find us anyway

S: I feel safer waiting in the branches up here

E: I'm going to try to run

A: If you run faster than Shah, the tiger won't catch you

H: Let's wait; maybe he will go away

E: If we wait much longer I might fall

AS TOLD

55. Less responsibility, less effort, less failure

H: How can I help?

S: Go and gather branches for the fire

H: I can do that

S: Bring some water, the bushes have caught fire

E: Shah, you brought too many branches!

H: I just did as I was told

A: You can't be bothered to think

S: It's my fault. I chose the wrong site

A: What can we expect from beginners?

56. More reliable more protected

S: Please take the boxes inside

A: I have better things to do

H: I will do it

S: You are always there for me

E: Shah is clumsy and drops things half the time

H: Oops! I slipped

E: Why did you ask Shah?

S: Shah, if you are hurt, we will take care of you

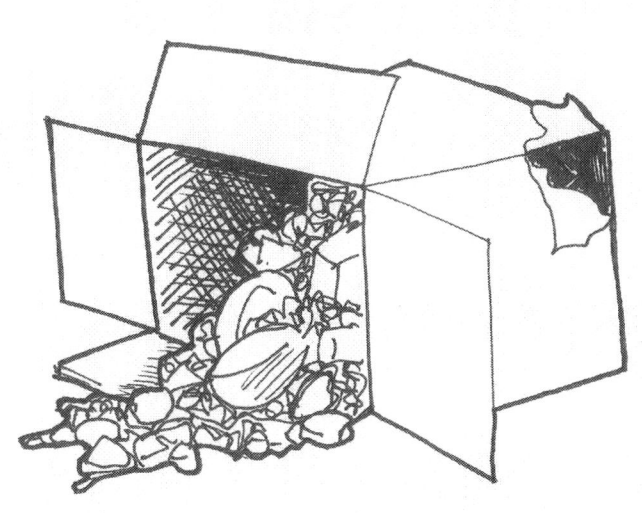

57. Habit, tradition and convention

A: Why did you kiss him on the cheek?

H: I am just saying hello

S: We do it whenever we meet

E: Is it to check if he's had a bath recently?

A: Maybe that's where the tradition comes from

E: We should consider doing the same

A: It might be awkward when we meet, if we haven't agreed it

E: It just looks silly

AS SEE FIT

58. Deciding

E: I want to go where the grass is green

S: Let's check the route on the Internet

A: The shepherd should know the best path

H: Does everyone have hiking boots?

E: Let's go then

A: If we take the most common path we won't get lost

H: Let's walk by the river, and maybe we can stop for a swim

E: Let's toss a coin to decide and see what happens!

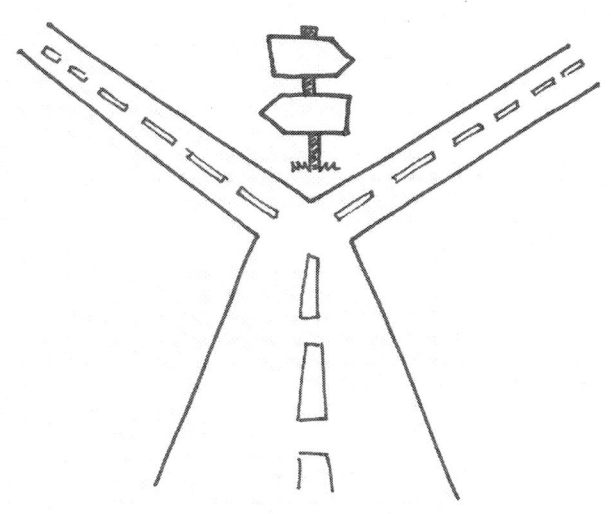

59. Taking risks and success

H: Let's pick cherries

A: There are only a few on the lower branches

E: Stand on my shoulders and look higher up

A: I could fall and hurt myself

H: If we don't take risks, we won't get many

A: That's easy to say when you are just watching

S: The ones on the ground have worms in them

E: Look, that tree has lots on the lower branches!

60. Savings and sacrifice

S: I am going to spend my last coins in the arcade

E: We have time now

A: Good idea! Coins are worth less every day

H: We could invest, earn a return and have more coins in the future

S: I should be studying instead of being here

E: I hurt myself when I stray from the library

H: What a waste

A: Suki, do as you see fit

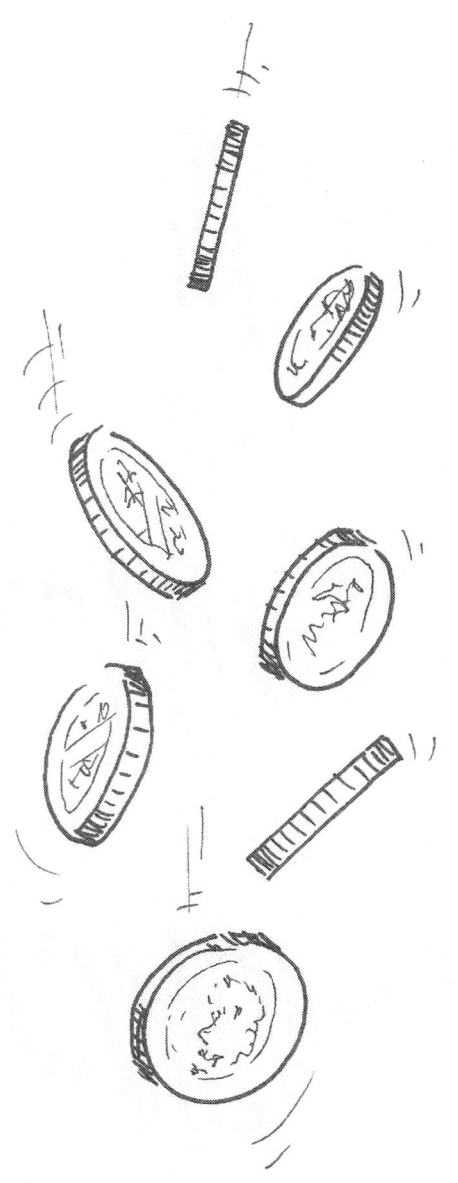

61. Performing

A: I would like to sing on a big stage one day

H: You were very good during practice

A: My voice cracks under pressure sometimes

E: Rehearsing will improve your confidence

S: We are not machines

E: Making mistakes is part of the fun

H: If I sang I would look like a fool

S: You would be most entertaining

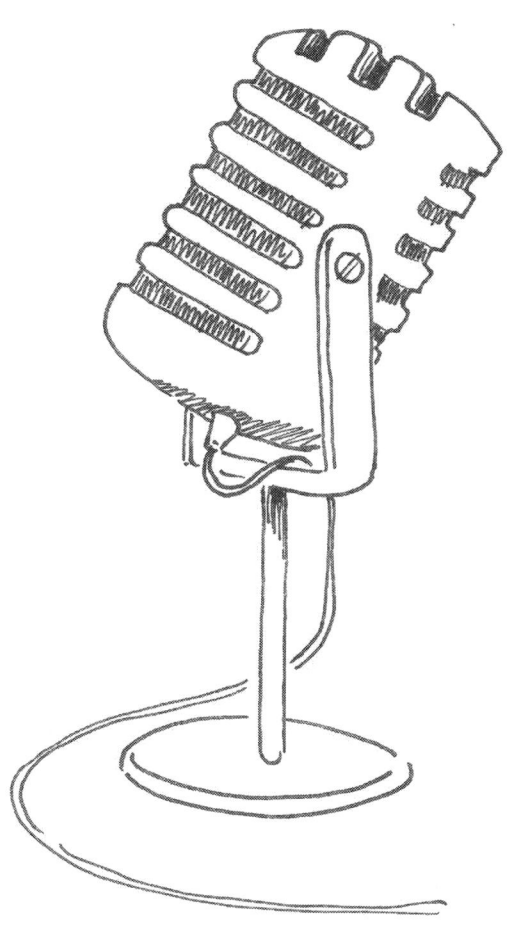

62. Rules and ethics

E: Don't hack my email account

S: Who says?

H: The law

A: If you break the law, there will be consequences

S: Only if I get caught

A: Laws can be wrong

E: It is wrong to hack my account, regardless of what the law says

H: Treat others as you want to be treated

63. Bullies and power

H: Stop drawing

A: You are trying to scare her so she won't win the drawing competition

S: You might as well take her pencil case

E: It is wrong and against the law

H: What are you going to do? I am stronger than you

A: Together we will teach him a lesson

S: It would be wrong to beat him up

E: We must punish him

PART III
RECOGNISING

WHY DO I COMPLAIN?

UNFAIRNESS

64. Unfairness

S: We agreed the winner keeps the poker set

E: Did you win?

S: I did, but Ani has taken it from me. It's not fair

H: There is no point in complaining

E: If we had proof, we could set things right

A: Every time I play with Suki, I lose

E: Very suspicious

A: Of course it is! Suki is a cheat!

LAMENT

65. Criticism and failure

A: The film was rubbish

S: You always criticise everything

E: Next time choose a better film

H: The reviews were not accurate

A: We should ask for our money back

S: We took our chances and got it wrong

A: (Cries) I am staying home from now on

E: Some people queued for an hour and didn't get in

S: Let's get over it and learn from this

66. Partial success

E: I am never going to be the best golfer in the world

A: That's the case for most people

H: How about the best in your neighbourhood?

S: You can't make a living from that

E: At least it keeps me fit

H: I win at golf on my computer by adjusting the level

A: That's pretty cool

H: Whatever makes you happy

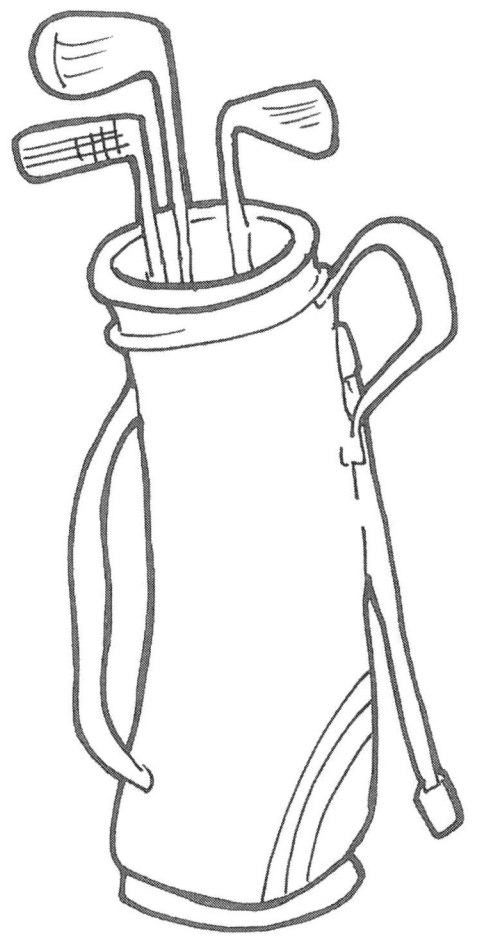

67. Getting back on your feet

H: I haven't finished a race in while

E: Perhaps you should stop riding

H: I have invested so much time, and now I keep falling over

A: You push yourself too hard

S: Don't give up!

A: If you change your technique, your odds will improve

S: Everyone goes through a bad patch at some point

H: I am so lucky to have your support

WHY DO I CELEBRATE?

WHY DO I CELEBRATE?

68. Celebration as acknowledgment

S: I finished the sandcastle!

H: That deserves a celebration

A: I don't think it's a big achievement. The beach is full of them

E: Suki is proud of it

A: When you build a real castle, I will celebrate with you

S: You don't want to acknowledge my achievement in front of others

A: You think everything you do is important and should be celebrated

H: Suki, I think you are great!

69. Partying

A: Are you ready to party?

S: Let's celebrate finishing the term!

H: It will be fun to dance and forget all that went wrong

E: For a bit you might feel you like passed your exams

S: We might meet lots of interesting people

H: And not as boring as those in the library

E: We can be as loud as we want

S: And we can plan the next party!

END

Printed in Great Britain
by Amazon

46494958R00102